ISEE QUICK RE\

MW00655551

Welcome, students and parents! This gu
the most essential content, strategies, ar.
Ivy Global also offers a full set of ISEE books: ISEE English, ISEE Math, and ISEE
Practice, in addition to SSAT & ISEE Vocabulary guides. These products are available
for purchase at isee.ivyglobal.com or amazon.com.

This publication was edited by the team at Ivy Global. The ISEE content was adapted
from the material in our ISEE Book Series.

Editors: Sacha Azor and Stephanie Bucklin
Producers: Lloyd Min and Junho Suh

Contributors: Corwin Henville, Lei Huang, Nathan Létourneau, Adam Wolsky, and
Nicole Young

ABOUT IVY GLOBAL

Ivy Global is a pioneering education company that delivers a wide range of
educational services.

E-mail: publishing@ivyglobal.com
Website: http://www.ivyglobal.com

Copyright 2015 by Ivy Global. All rights reserved.

ISEE is a registered trademark of the Educational Records Bureau, which is not
affiliated with this book.

ABOUT THE ISEE

The ISEE (Independent School Entrance Exam) consists of four scored sections (**Verbal Reasoning, Quantitative Reasoning, Reading Comprehension**, and **Mathematics Achievement**), plus an **Essay**. The essay isn't scored, but is shared with the schools that you are applying to so that they may use it as a writing sample. The format of the test differs based on the level of the exam:

LOWER LEVEL			
Section	Questions	Length	Topics Covered
Verbal Reasoning	34	20 min	Synonyms, Sentence Completion
Quantitative Reasoning	38	35 min	Logical Reasoning, Pattern Recognition (Word Problems)
Reading Comprehension	25	25 min	Short Passages
Math Achievement	30	30 min	Arithmetic, Algebra, Geometry, Data Analysis
Essay	1	30 min	One age-appropriate essay prompt
Total testing time: 2 hours 20 minutes			

MIDDLE AND UPPER LEVEL			
Section	Questions	Length	Topics Covered
Verbal Reasoning	40	20 min	Synonyms, Sentence Completion
Quantitative Reasoning	37	35 min	Logical Reasoning, Pattern Recognition (Word Problems and Quantitative Comparison)
Reading Comprehension	36	35 min	Short Passages
Math Achievement	47	40 min	Arithmetic, Algebra, Geometry, Data Analysis
Essay	1	30 min	One age-appropriate essay prompt
Total testing time: 2 hours 40 minutes			

Except for the Essay, all questions are multiple-choice (A) to (D). You are not normally allowed to use calculators, rulers, dictionaries, or other aids during the exam. However, students with documented learning disabilities or physical challenges may apply to take the test with extra time, aids, or other necessary accommodations that they receive in school. For more information about taking the ISEE with a documented disability, visit the ISEE Website at ERBlearn.org.

GRIDDING ANSWER CHOICES

On a computer-based exam, you will click an answer on the computer screen in order to enter your response. Follow the directions carefully to make sure your answer has been recorded. Within each section, you will be able to go back to questions earlier in the section and change your answers. You will also be able to skip questions and come back to them later.

On a pencil-and-paper exam, you will enter your answers on a separate answer sheet. You must grid in your multiple-choice answers onto this sheet using an HB or #2 pencil to fill in the circle that corresponds to your answer. This sheet is scanned and scored by a highly sensitive computer. You will also write your Essay on separate lined pages of this answer sheet. Keep your answer sheet neat and avoid stray marks. In the graphic, Answer 6 shows the correct way to input your answers.

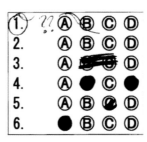

IMPORTANT NOTES

SCORING

- All of the multiple-choice questions on the ISEE are equal in value.
- There is no penalty for incorrect answers, so you should always guess.

STRATEGIES

1. Grid your answer choices correctly and carefully. **Try gridding your answers in batches of four, five, or six answer choices.** That way, you do not have to go back and forth between your test booklet and answer sheet every minute.
2. **Pace yourself** to manage your time effectively.
3. Learn a strategic approach for multiple-choice questions.
   a. **Make predictions**: Try to come up with an answer on your own before looking at the answer choices.
4. Use Process of Elimination.
5. **Try back-solving**: In math sections, instead of writing an equation, try plugging in the answer choices to the word problem.

Verbal Reasoning

Synonym Strategies

- Start by covering up the answer choices and thinking of your own definition for the word in capital letters.
- Come up with contexts—phrases where you might have heard the word before. A word's context is everything in a phrase or sentence that might influence the word's meaning.
- Think of the word's connotation—its secondary meaning, or the feeling we get from the word. A word can have a positive connotation if it means something good, a negative connotation if it means something bad, or a neutral connotation if it is neither good nor bad.

Sentence Completion Strategies

1. Select the word that would make the most sense with the entire sentence.
2. LOOK FOR CLUES
   a. Start by covering up the answer choices and reading the entire sentence to yourself, skipping over the blanks. Try to get a sense of the sentence's main message, even with the missing words.
   b. Then, think of a way that you might complete the sentence. Circle or underline clues nearby in the sentence that could help you identify what type of words should go in the blanks.
3. WRITE YOUR OWN WORDS
   a. When you have an idea of what types of words could complete the sentence, write them down.
   b. Then, uncover the answer choices and look for an answer that matches the word or words you wrote down.
4. PLUG IT IN
   a. When you have chosen a likely answer for the question, the last step is to test your answer by plugging it in to the rest of the sentence to make sure that it fits.
   b. In order to be completely sure that you have chosen the best answer, plug in all of the other choices as well. This will help you make sure that you have really chosen the best fit for the entire sentence.

TYPES OF CLUES

Identifying clues in each sentence completion question will help you pick the one correct answer choice to complete the sentence. When you are looking for these clues, you'll want to pay attention to certain types of words that provide information about the structure and tone of the sentence.

DEFINITIONS AND SYNONYMS

When you are reading a sentence, pay close attention to any part of the sentence that provides a definition or synonym of the missing words or phrases.

TONE WORDS

When you are looking for clues, pay attention to any positive or negative words in the sentence. These might tell you something about the tone of the sentence, which can help you decide whether the missing word or phrase should be positive, negative, or neutral.

TRANSITION WORDS

Transition words are important clues that tell you how the sentence is structured: they let you know whether part of the sentence supports an earlier statement, contrasts with what came before, or shows cause and effect. Looking for transition words will help you decide what words or phrases would fit best with the structure of the sentence as a whole.

Transition Words	
Type	Examples
Support	and, in addition, as well as, furthermore, likewise, similarly, moreover
Contrast	but, yet, however, though, although, even, though, despite, instead, rather, nonetheless
Cause and Effect	because, so, therefore, thus, consequently, as a result, in order to, since

PHRASE RESPONSES: LOWER LEVEL ONLY

On the Lower Level test, the last 6 sentence completion questions of the Verbal Reasoning section will be **phrase responses**, which ask you to complete a sentence with a full phrase, rather than a word or two.

Questions are the same level of difficulty as other sentence completion questions. Look for transition words that tell you something about the sentence structure, and then pick an answer that is the best fit for that structure.

PAIRED WORD RESPONSES: UPPER LEVEL ONLY

On the Upper Level test, the last 9 questions of the Verbal Reasoning section will be paired word responses. Instead of filling in one blank in the sentence, these questions ask you to fill in **two** blanks. The answer choices will be pairs of words, and you will need to select the answer choices where both words are the best fit for the whole sentence.

Paired word responses are slightly more complicated than other sentence completion questions, but the process for solving them is the same:

1. Look for clues in the sentence that will help you guess what type of words should go in the blanks.
2. Pay close attention to any words in the sentence that point to a certain relationship between the two words.
3. Take a look at your answer choices. Eliminate any answers that don't fit in the first blank, and only look at the remaining answers to decide which word would fit in the second blank.

IF YOU GET STUCK

- If you don't know a word, try using your knowledge of **context** to guess at a relationship.
- Remember that you are looking for the best fit, which may be an answer choice with an unfamiliar word.
- For the whole ISEE exam, you should always guess. Never leave a question on the ISEE blank! Remember to use the Process of Elimination to narrow down your answer options and increase your odds of guessing the right answer. Then, take your best guess and move on.

READING COMPREHENSION

APPROACHING THE READING SECTION

- Focus on the shorter passages first and save the long passages for last.
- Read quickly: try to understand main points rather than small details.
- Answer questions about the main idea or the main purpose first, and then turn to questions that ask about specific details in the passage.
- Underline the key words and transitional words.
- Try to guess the meaning of unfamiliar words **in context**, by looking for clues nearby.
- Practice building your vocabulary before the test.

TYPES OF PASSAGES

1. Informative passages: explain or describe a main topic. (Ex: articles in an encyclopedia, textbook, or even a newspaper)
2. Persuasive passages: convince the reader of a specific position or argument. (Ex: political speech, opinion essay, newspaper op-ed)
   a. Try to imagine who is speaking and who his or her intended audience might be.
   b. Pay close attention to the author's **tone**. Because a persuasive passage presents an opinion, the author will frequently have a **positive** or **negative** feeling about the topic she is discussing.
3. Narrative passages: tell a story about an event or an experience (Ex: autobiography, memoir)
   a. Figure out if the narrative is from the first-person point of view or the third-person point of view.
   b. The **theme** of a narrative is its "main idea," or the message it conveys about life and behavior.

TYPES OF QUESTIONS

1. Main idea questions: ask about the author's main topic, theme, or thesis.
   a. Pay close attention to the first and last sentences of the passage, because they frequently give you information about its main idea.
   b. Eliminate answer options that are **too broad** or **too specific**.
2. Supporting idea questions: ask you to identify specific information mentioned in the passage.

a. **Go back to the passage** to see where you might find the information you need.

b. If you are not given a line number where you can find the answer, first **underline** the main points in the question, and then **skim** the passage to find this information.

c. Only base your answer off of what the author says in the passage.

3. Inference questions: ask you to make a logical guess or assumption based on the information in the passage—analyzing what is implied but not directly stated.

a. Pick an answer choice that best matches the author's primary purpose in the passage.

b. Eliminate answers that are unrelated to the main idea of the passage, or that aren't supported by the **author's own words**.

4. Vocabulary questions: ask you to define a word as it is used in the context of the passage.

a. The word will often have **multiple possible meanings**—pick the definition that best matches how the author uses the word in a certain sentence.

b. Some questions may ask you to define **tricky vocabulary** like old-fashioned words or technical terms. Look at the context of these words, including surrounding sentences, for clues.

5. Organization/logic questions: ask you to identify information about the structure, argument, and function of the passage.

a. Identify the author's **main point** or **purpose** to determine how different components of the passage work together to convey that main idea.

b. **Re-read the relevant section of the passage carefully** and think about how it helps the author make his overall point in the passage.

c. To find the author's **evidence**, identify the main points in the passage, and then look for the supporting information that serves as "proof" for these points.

d. Pay close attention to the words **NOT**, **LEAST**, and **EXCEPT** in the questions.

6. Tone/style/figurative language questions: ask you to analyze *how* the author is writing.

a. **Tone:** the author's attitude toward the topic—neutral, emotionally involved, etc.

b. **Style** or **mood:** how the passage evokes certain emotions or images

c. **Figurative language:** the author's use of images, metaphors, and other rhetorical devices, often to add heightened meaning or to create a particular **mood**

i.   **Imagery:** uses descriptive words from the five senses to create a vivid image in the reader's mind—"a fiery blaze of gold"

ii. **Symbol:** a word that represents another concept or idea within a poem—for example, an author talking about spring in order to symbolize renewal

iii. **Simile:** a device that compares two things using "like" or "as"—"His laugh was like a thunderclap"

iv. **Personification:** a technique that gives human characteristics to animals, objects, or ideas—"Winter jealously steals the world's warmth"

d. **The style of the passage** often matches the tone. If you have trouble finding the tone, look for any **positive or negative words** that might indicate the author's opinion about the topic.

Tone Words	
Type	Examples
Positive	admiring, appreciative, assertive, authoritative, celebratory, enthusiastic, empathetic, exuberant, jubilant, impassioned, lighthearted, passionate, reverent
Negative	bitter, critical, condescending, concerned, contemptuous, cynical, disparaging, dubious, harsh, hostile, indignant, outraged, skeptical, somber
Humorous	amused, comical, flippant, ironic, mocking, sarcastic, satiric
Neutral	ambivalent, analytical, apathetic, detached, disinterested, indifferent, informative, matter-of-fact, objective, unbiased, unconcerned, unemotional

Symbol	Meaning
sleep	death
dreams	fate, the future
light (sun, stars, moon)	good, hope, freedom
dark	evil, magic, the unknown
spring	youth, birth, life
winter	death, dying, old age
owl	wisdom
dove	peace
rose	love, beauty
crown	wealth, royalty
ring	love, commitment

VOCABULARY BUILDING

QUICK TIPS

Learn **all possible meanings** of new words and see how they are **used in a sentence**.

Come up with a **personal trigger** to help you build a personal connection with the word.

Come up with a **wacky way to remember the word** based on what it sounds like.

Use **flashcards** to help you learn and **practice** using new words frequently.

COMMON WORD ROOTS, PREFIXES, AND SUFFIXES

Common Roots		
Root	Meaning	Examples
ag, act	do	action, activity, agent
ami, amo	love	amiable, amorous
anim	mind, soul, spirit	animal, animate, unanimous
auto	self	autobiography, autograph
ben	good	beneficial, benevolence
bio	life	biography, biology
chron	time	chronic, chronology, synchronize
corp	body	corporation, corporeal, corpse
dic, dict	speak	dictate, contradict
err	wander	error, erratic, errand
luc	light	elucidate, lucid, translucent
magn	great	magnify, magnanimous
mal	bad	malevolent, malicious
nov	new	novice, innovate, renovate
omni	all	omniscient, omnipotent
phil	love	philanthropist, philosophy
poten	able, powerful	potential, omnipotent, impotent
terr	land	terrain, terrestrial, subterranean
ver	truth	veracity, verify, veracious
viv, vit	alive	revival, vivacious, vitality

Common Prefixes

Prefix	Meaning	Examples
an, a	without	anarchy, amoral
anti	against	antipathy, antisocial
co, col, com, con	with, together	coauthor, collaborate
contra, contro	against	contradict, contravene, controversy
di, dif, dis	not, apart	digress, differ, disparity
e, ex, extra, extro	out, beyond	expel, extrovert, eject
in, il, im, ir (1)	not	inefficient, illegible
in, il, im, ir (2)	in, upon	invite, illuminate, impression
inter	between, among	intervene, interjection
mono	one	monarchy, monologue, monotheism
mis	bad, hatred	misdemeanor, misanthrope
non	not, without	nonentity, nondescript
pan	all, every	panacea, panorama, pandemic
post	after	postpone, posterity
pre	before	preamble, premonition
sub, suc, sup, sus	under, less	subway, subjugate, suppress
trans	across	transfer, transpose
un	not	unabridged, unkempt

Common Suffixes

Suffix	Meaning	Examples
able, ible	ADJ: capable of	edible, presentable
ac, ic, ical	ADJ: like, related	cardiac, mythic, dramatic
acious, icious	ADJ: full of	malicious, audacious
ant, ent	ADJ/N: full of	eloquent, verdant
ate	V: make, become	consecrate, eradicate
cy, ty, ity	N: state of being	democracy, veracity
ful	ADJ: full of	respectful, cheerful, wonderful
fy	V: to make	magnify, petrify, beautify
ism	N: doctrine, belief	monotheism, fanaticism, egoism
ize, ise	V: make	victimize, rationalize, harmonize
logy	N: study of	biology, geology, neurology
tion, sion	N: state of being	exasperation, irritation
tude	N: state of	fortitude, beautitude, certitude

THE ESSAY

Plan to spend no more than a few minutes choosing your prompt, brainstorming, and planning, and save a few minutes at the end to edit.

QUICK WRITING TIPS

- Use the author's full name the first time you use it (you can just use his or her last name after).
- Be **specific**. Keep your writing clear and to the point.
- **Write descriptively** by using sensory descriptions, identifying key characteristics of your subject, and describing/explaining causes and effects.
- **Indent** your paragraphs and use proper **capitalization**.
- Avoid using phrases like "a lot" and "really."
- Avoid the passive voice—Ex: Write "Joe wrote the essay" (active voice) instead of "The essay was written by Joe" (passive voice).
- Avoid run-on sentences.

Selected Punctuation		
Type	Description	Example
commas	most frequently used to join together two clauses (parts) of a sentence, often before conjunctions; also used before and after descriptive phrases in a sentence, and between three or more items in a list	After Sarah, Emily, and Xiwen finished their paper, they celebrated with ice cream.
colons	used to introduce examples or items in a list	Elaine has three daughters: Amy, Michaela, and Christine.
semicolons	used to join together complete sentences without a comma or conjunction	Victoria was frequently tardy; therefore, she received a low grade.
parentheses	used to provide extra information in a sentence	In case of an emergency, exit through the north doors (next to the principal's office).
hyphens	used in compound words and numbers	Susan's ex-husband was a well-known author.

STRUCTURE

1. Introduction: a single paragraph outlining your position and containing your **thesis statement**
2. Body: 2-3 paragraphs describing different reasons or examples that explains your position
   a. **Use relevant details** and **analyze your examples** to show how they support your position.
   b. **Transition** into your next body paragraph with a short phrase that links it to your previous point.
3. Conclusion: a final paragraph summarizing your position and argument for the reader

TYPES OF ESSAYS

1. A **descriptive essay**: requires you to describe or define characteristics or qualities.
   a. Stick to what you know.
   b. Choose two to three qualities you'd like to discuss and explain how they relate to your subject.
2. A **persuasive essay**: requires you to argue for or against an idea, urge the reader to act a certain way, or convince the reader to agree with a certain position on an issue
   a. Clearly state your thesis statement in the introduction.
   b. Use concrete, specific examples to support your position, including history, science, literature, current events, or well-described personal examples.
   c. Restate your thesis in your conclusion.
   d. Upper Level Strategy: Conclude your essay by refuting (disproving) a counterargument.
3. A **cause and effect essay**: requires you to describe a situation and analyze its possible causes and effects.
   a. Identify causes, explain effects, and offer solutions.
   b. Explain how things can be done differently to improve the situation.
   c. Narrate possibilities and show potential outcomes.

QUANTITATIVE REASONING

TIPS

- Write down your work on the scratch paper provided.
- Break complicated problems into steps and tackle one step at a time.
- Use figures and diagrams provided (though note they are not necessarily drawn to scale unless the question says otherwise), or draw your own figure to help you organize your thoughts and information.
- Check your work.

STRATEGIES

- **Guess and check**: Especially with **geometry** problems or problems where a diagram is given, you can narrow your choices down to one based on what seems reasonable, or try rounding to come to an approximate answer.
- **Process of Elimination:** Eliminate any answer options that you know are wrong.
- **Picking numbers**: For **algebra** questions that contain a lot of variables, you can often pick an easy number to work with and plug this into the equation.
- **Back-solving**: Work backwards from the multiple-choice answers you are given. Only use back-solving if the answer choices don't include variables.
  - o Hint: answer choices that are numbers are often given in order (smallest to largest, or largest to smallest). Start by plugging in the middle answer. If it doesn't work, you can determine whether to try a larger or smaller answer.

WORD PROBLEMS

APPROACHES

- Read through the entire question carefully. Underline or circle **key words**.
- Ask yourself, "What is the question asking me to solve?"
- Draw a **chart** or **diagram** to help you visualize the problem, if applicable.

Quantitative comparison questions give you values in two columns, Column A and Column B, and ask you to compare these values and select one of the following multiple-choice answers:

(A) The quantity in Column A is greater.

(B) The quantity in Column B is greater.

(C) The two quantities are equal.

(D) The relationship cannot be determined from the information given.

Example:

Column A	Column B
$x + 8$	$2x + 2$

(Correct Answer: D—It is not possible to determine which quantity is greater without knowing the value of x.)

APPROACHES

- **Simplify** the values in each column. You could also add, subtract, multiply, or divide the same number by the values in **both columns**.
  - Caution: You can **only multiply or divide both columns by a positive number**, because the two columns might represent two sides of an inequality, and multiplying or dividing by a negative number would reverse the inequality.
- Pay attention to **which variables** appear in each column. If the columns contain different variables, they may stand for different numbers.
- If you get stuck on a question involving algebra, try **plugging in numbers** to the expressions you are given.
  - **Zero** is often a good number to plug in.
  - However, you should never pick an answer choice without testing some extreme values (including large numbers, decimals, negative numbers, etc.). Make sure to test enough values to eliminate wrong answer choices and locate the correct answer.
- Look for **shortcuts** by estimating or making a smart guess.

MATH ACHIEVEMENT

Arithmetic Review		
Name	Definition	Examples
Integer	any positive or negative whole number	−3, 1, 200
Operation	a process that changes one number into another	+, −, ×, ÷
Even Number	divisible by 2	2, 4, 6, 8…
Odd number	not divisible by 2	1, 3, 5, 7…
Sum	the result of adding numbers	The sum of 3 and 4 is 7
Difference	the result of subtracting numbers	The difference between 5 and 2 is 3
Product	the result of multiplying numbers	The product of 6 and 4 is 24
Quotient	the result of dividing numbers	The quotient when 40 is divided by 5 is 8
Remainder	the amount left over when a number cannot be evenly divided by another number	When 11 is divided by 2, the result is 5 with a remainder of 1
Property of Commutation	$a + b = b + a$ $a \times b = b \times a$	$3 + 1 = 1 + 3$ $2 \times 7 = 7 \times 2$
Property of Association	$a + (b + c) = (a + b) + c$ $a \times (b \times c) = (a \times b) \times c$	$3 + (4 + 2) = (3 + 4) + 2$ $5 \times (2 \times 3) = (5 \times 2) \times 3$
Property of Distribution	$a(b + c) = ab + ac$	$5 (2 + 4) = 10 + 20 = 30$
Factor	a number that another number is evenly divisible by	3 is a factor of 12
Multiple	a number that can be divided evenly by the original	12 is a multiple of 3
Prime Number	has only 2 factors: 1 and itself	2, 3, 5, 7, 11, 13, 17…
Composite Number	has more than 2 factors	4, 6, 9, 10, 12, 15…
Prime Factors	prime numbers that, when multiplied, give the original number	3, 3, and 2 for 12
Greatest Common Factor (GCF)	largest integer that is a factor of both given integers	8 is the GCF of 16 and 24
Least Common Multiple (LCM)	smallest integer that is a multiple of both given integers	48 is the LCM of 16 and 24
Patterns	lists that follow a rule	

Sequence	a pattern involving numbers (called terms)	5, 7, 9, 11, 13... or 5, 10, 20, 40, 80...
Positive Numbers	greater than zero	1, 2, 3, 4, 5...
Negative Numbers	less than zero; negative sign in front	$-1, -2, -3, -4, -5...$
Imaginary Numbers (Upper Level Only)	a number that does not exist in the set of real numbers	$\sqrt{-1}$, often represented as i

For more information, refer to the Ivy Global ISEE Math Guide (see pages 134-167).

ORDER OF OPERATIONS: MIDDLE/UPPER LEVEL ONLY

PEMDAS: (Parentheses, Exponents, Multiplication and Division, Addition and Subtraction)

$$Ex: \quad 5 \times (4 + 5) + 2^3 - 4 \div 2$$
$$5 \times (9) + 8 - 2$$
$$45 + 8 - 2$$
$$51$$

FRACTIONS, RATIOS, DECIMALS, AND PERCENTS

Converting Between Fractions, Decimals, and Percents: ML/UL Only		
Operation	Explanation	Example
Fraction $\longrightarrow$ Decimal	divide the numerator by the denominator using long division	$\frac{1}{4} = 0.25$
Fraction $\longrightarrow$ Percent	convert the fraction into a decimal using long division, then multiply by 100%	$\frac{1}{4} = 25\%$
Decimal $\longrightarrow$ Fraction	rewrite your decimal as a fraction with a denominator of 10, 100, or 1000 (depending how many digits are after the dot) and simplify	$0.4 = \frac{4}{10} = \frac{2}{5}$
Decimal $\longrightarrow$ Percent	multiply by 100 and add a % sign	$0.4 = 40\%$
Percent $\longrightarrow$ Fraction	put percent as the numerator and 100 as the denominator and simplify	$35\% = \frac{35}{100} = \frac{7}{20}$
Percent $\longrightarrow$ Decimal	divide by 100 and remove % sign	$35\% = 0.35$

CONVERTING BETWEEN RATIOS AND FRACTIONS

A **ratio** represents a relationship between 2 or more parts. Both numbers in a ratio make up the whole. If a ratio of one part to another part is expressed in a fraction, you can write another fraction expressing one part to the whole by adding the numerator and the denominator of the original fraction and making it the denominator of your new fraction.

Ex: The ratio of boys to girls in a class is $\frac{2}{3}$. What is the fraction of boys in the class?

$$\frac{2}{2+3} = \frac{2}{5}$$

Fractions		
Category	Description	Examples
Mixed Number	combination of a whole number and a fraction	$3\frac{1}{2}$
Improper Fraction	fraction where the numerator is bigger than the denominator	$\frac{11}{5}$
Adding and Subtracting Fractions	convert fractions into equivalents (same denominator) and perform operations on numerator	$\frac{1}{7} + \frac{2}{7} = \frac{3}{7}$
Multiplying Fractions	multiply the numerators and denominators separately	$\frac{1}{4} \times \frac{3}{5} = \frac{3}{20}$
Dividing Fractions	multiply by the reciprocal of the second fraction	$\frac{1}{4} \div \frac{3}{5} = \frac{1}{4} \times \frac{5}{3} = \frac{5}{12}$
Cross-Multiplying (Middle/Upper Level Only)	If $\frac{a}{b} = \frac{c}{d}$ then $a \times d = c \times b$	$\frac{3}{5} = \frac{6}{10}$ $3 \times 10 = 6 \times 5$

For more information, refer to the Ivy Global ISEE Math Guide (see pages 168-206).

Exponent Rules: UL Only	
Rule	Example
$a^1 = a$	$8^1 = 8$
$a^0 = 1$	$8^0 = 1$
$a^{-m} = \frac{1}{a^m}$	$8^{-2} = \frac{1}{8^2} = \frac{1}{64}$
$a^{\frac{1}{m}} = \sqrt[m]{a}$	$8^{\frac{1}{3}} = \sqrt[3]{8} = 2$
$a^m a^n = a^{m+n}$	$8^2 \times 8^3 = 8^{2+3} = 8^5 = 32768$
$\frac{a^m}{a^n} = a^{m-n}$	$\frac{8^3}{8^2} = 8^{3-2} = 8^1 = 8$
$(a^m)^n = a^{mn}$	$(8^2)^3 = 8^{2 \times 3} = 8^6 = 262144$
$a^m b^m = (ab)^m$	$8^3 \times 2^3 = (8 \times 2)^3 = 16^3 = 4096$

$\dfrac{a^m}{b^m} = \left(\dfrac{a}{b}\right)^m$	$\dfrac{8^3}{2^3} = \left(\dfrac{8}{2}\right)^3 = 4^3 = 64$
$a^{\frac{m}{n}} = \sqrt[n]{a^m}$	$8^{\frac{2}{3}} = \sqrt[3]{8^2} = \sqrt[3]{64} = 4$
$\sqrt{ab} = \sqrt{a} \times \sqrt{b}$	$\sqrt{16 \times 4} = \sqrt{16} \times \sqrt{4} = 4 \times 2 = 8$
$\sqrt{\dfrac{a}{b}} = \dfrac{\sqrt{a}}{\sqrt{b}}$	$\sqrt{\dfrac{16}{4}} = \dfrac{\sqrt{16}}{\sqrt{4}} = \dfrac{4}{2} = 2$

Algebra Review: ML/UL Only

Name	Definition	Examples
Variable	represents number that is unknown	x, y, a
Algebraic expression	a mathematical "phrase" containing numbers, variables, and operations	$2x + 5$
Terms	variables and/or numbers multiplied together	$17, 2x, y$
Coefficient	number before a variable	In $9x$, the coefficient is "9"
Monomial	an expression with one term	$2x$
Binomial	an expression with two terms	$2x + y$
Polynomial	an expression with more than one term	$2x + y; 3y + 4z + 12x$
Like terms	expressions with the same variables raised to the same power; can be combined with + and − in expressions	$3x + 4x + x^2 = 7x + x^2$
Distributive property	$a(b + c) = ab + ac$	$3x\,(x + 4) = 3x^2 + 12x$
FOIL method (Upper Level Only)	$(a + b)(c + d) =$ $ac + ad + bc + bd$	$(x + 3)(x + 2)$ $x^2 + 2x + 3x + 6$ $x^2 + 5x + 6$
Factoring (Upper Level Only)	opposite of distribution; finding the greatest common factor all terms have in common	$6x^2 + 4x = 2x(3x + 2)$ $x^2 + 7x + 10 = (x + 5)(x + 2)$ $2y^2 - 11y + 12 = (y - 4)(2y - 3)$
Algebraic equation	tells you two expressions are equal to each other	$9x = 36$
Inequality	a mathematical statement comparing two unequal quantities	$4x + 7 < 15$
Solving inequalities	you can preserve the inequality while solving as a normal equation, EXCEPT when multiplying or dividing by a negative number, which reverses the inequality	$5 > 3$ $5 \times (-4) < 3 \times (-4)$ $-20 < -12$

Function	a formula that shows how one set of numbers or variables (**input**) is transformed into another set of numbers or variables (**output**)	input + 4 = output
Strange Symbols	stars, bubbles, smiley faces, etc., used to represent relationships among numbers and variables	For any numbers N and M, $N \blacklozenge M = 2N + 3M$
Absolute Value (Upper Level Only)	a number's distance away from zero on a number line	$\|-3\| = 3$
Absolute Value Equations	If $\|x\| = a$, then $x = a$ or $x = -a$	$\|x - 5\| = 4$ $x - 5 = 4$ and $x - 5 = -4$ $x = 9$ and $x = 1$
Absolute Value Inequality: <	If $\|x\| < a$, then $-a < x < a$	If $\|x\| < 3$, then $-3 < x < 3$
Absolute Value Inequality: >	If $\|x\| > a$, then $x < -a$ or $x > a$	If $\|x\| > 2$, then $x < -2$ or $x > 2$
Matrix (Upper Level Only)	a two-dimensional array of numbers, with both rows and columns	$\begin{bmatrix} 2 & -3 \\ 3 & 0 \\ 1 & 5 \end{bmatrix}$
Matrix Addition and Subtraction (Upper Level Only)	First, check whether two matrices have the same number of rows and columns. Next, add or subtract the corresponding values in each row and column.	$\begin{bmatrix} 2 & -3 \\ 3 & 0 \\ 1 & 5 \end{bmatrix} + \begin{bmatrix} 1 & -3 \\ 3 & 1 \\ 1 & 2 \end{bmatrix}$ $\begin{bmatrix} 2+1 & -3+(-3) \\ 3+3 & 0+1 \\ 1+1 & 5+2 \end{bmatrix}$ $\begin{bmatrix} 3 & -6 \\ 6 & 1 \\ 2 & 7 \end{bmatrix}$
Matrix Multiplication (Upper Level Only)	Multiply row by column: multiply the values in the row of the first matrix by the values in the columns of the second matrix in pairs. Then, add these products together.	$\begin{bmatrix} 3 & 4 \\ 2 & -1 \end{bmatrix} \times \begin{bmatrix} 0 & 5 \\ 1 & -2 \end{bmatrix}$ 1st value: 2nd value: $3 \times 0 = 0$ $3 \times 5 = 15$ $4 \times 1 = 4$ $4 \times (-2) = -8$ $0 + 4 = 4$ $15 + (-8) = 7$ 3rd value: 4th value: $2 \times 0 = 0$ $2 \times 5 = 10$ $-1 \times 1 = -1$ $-1 \times -2 = 2$ $0 + (-1) = -1$ $10 + 2 = 12$ $\begin{bmatrix} 4 & 7 \\ -1 & 12 \end{bmatrix}$

For more information, refer to the Ivy Global ISEE Math Guide (see pages 238-291).

GEOMETRY REVIEW

LINES

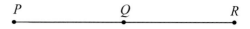

P and R are the **endpoints**.
Q is the **midpoint**.

ANGLES

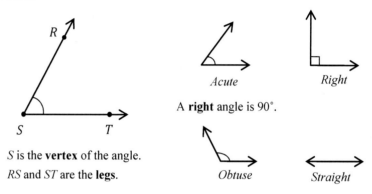

Acute

A **right** angle is 90°.

Right

S is the **vertex** of the angle.
RS and *ST* are the **legs**.

Obtuse

Straight

Two angles that have equal measures are called **congruent**.
A line that **bisects** an angle divides it into two equal parts.

TRANSVERSALS: UPPER LEVEL ONLY

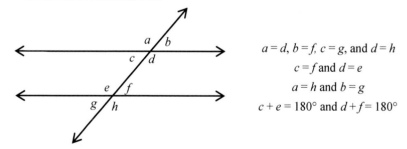

$a = d$, $b = f$, $c = g$, and $d = h$
$c = f$ and $d = e$
$a = h$ and $b = g$
$c + e = 180°$ and $d + f = 180°$

POLYGONS

The **perimeter** of any polygon is the distance around its sides.
Congruent polygons: have the same size and shape.
Similar polygons: have the same shape, but not the same size.

Angles of a Triangle

The sum of the interior angles of a triangle is 180°

Equilateral   *Isosceles*   *Scalene*   *Right*

Pythagorean Theorem for right triangles (Upper Level Only):

$$a^2 + b^2 = c^2$$

Trigonometry (Upper Level Only): SOHCAHTOA

$\sin(\theta)$:	$\cos(\theta)$:	$\tan(\theta)$:
$\dfrac{\text{opposite}}{\text{hypotenuse}}$	$\dfrac{\text{adjacent}}{\text{hypotenuse}}$	$\dfrac{\text{opposite}}{\text{adjacent}}$

QUADRILATERALS: MIDDLE/UPPER LEVEL ONLY

Parallelogram

Area = base × height

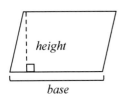

Rectangle

Area = length × width

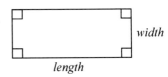

Square

Area = side²

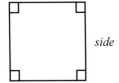

Trapezoid

$$Area = \frac{1}{2} \times height \times (base\ 1 + base\ 2)$$

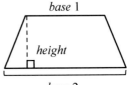

Kite

Area = (total height × base) ÷ 2

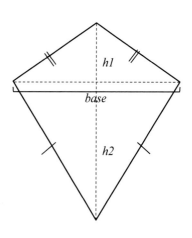

Net

(any unfolded three-dimensional shape)

Cube *C*

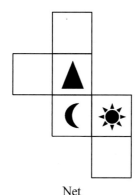

Net

CIRCLES: MIDDLE/UPPER LEVEL ONLY

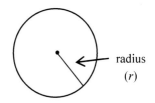

radius
(*r*)

Diameter = $2r$

Circumference = πd or $2\pi r$

Area = πr^2

Circle = 360°

SOLID GEOMETRY

Prisms (Middle/Upper Level Only)

Volume = length × width × height

Surface area = sum of the areas of all faces

Cylinders (Upper Level Only)

Volume = $\pi \times r^2 \times height$

Surface area =
(area of both bases) + *(circumference × height)*

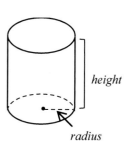

height

radius

Spheres (Upper Level Only)

$$Volume = \frac{4}{3}\pi r^3$$

$$Surface\ area = 4\pi r^2$$

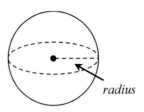

radius

Pyramids (Upper Level Only)

$$Volume = \frac{1}{3}\ (base\ area) \times height$$

$$Surface\ area =$$

$$base\ area + \frac{base\ perimeter \times slant\ height}{2}$$

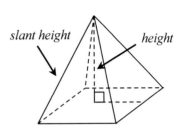

slant height   height

Cones (Upper Level Only)

$$Volume = \frac{1}{3}\ (base\ area) \times height$$

$$Surface\ area =$$

$$\pi \times r^2 + \pi \times r \times slant\ height$$

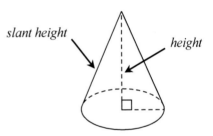

slant height   height

COORDINATE GEOMETRY REVIEW

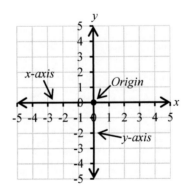

Ordered pair: (x, y)

GRAPHS OF FUNCTIONS: MIDDLE/UPPER LEVEL ONLY

To graph a function, we represent the first set of data points along the x axis and the second set of data points along the y axis.

A linear **function** is a function that has a constant rate of change, represented on a graph as a straight line.

$$y = mx + b$$

m is the **slope** (rate of change)

b is the y-intercept

Determining Slope		
Type	Rule	Example
Any line on a graph	$m = \frac{\text{rise}}{\text{run}} = \frac{y_2 - y_1}{x_2 - x_1}$	For line with points (0, 0) and (5, 10), slope is $\frac{10-0}{5-0} = \frac{10}{5} = 13$
Horizontal line	$m = 0$	$y = 2$
Vertical line	m = undefined	$x = 5$
Parallel lines	m is the same for both lines	$y = 2x + 4$ and $y = 2x - 7$
Perpendicular lines	Product of the two slopes is -1 (if one slope is m, the other is $\frac{-1}{m}$)	$y = 5x + 3$ and $y = -\frac{1}{5}x + 12$

For more information, refer to the Ivy Global ISEE Math Guide (see pages 306-406).

DATA INTERPRETATION REVIEW

Pictographs

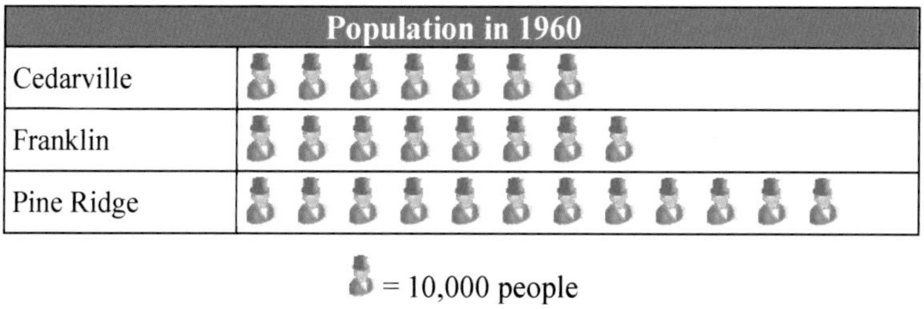

Population in 1960
Cedarville
Franklin
Pine Ridge
= 10,000 people

Bar Graphs

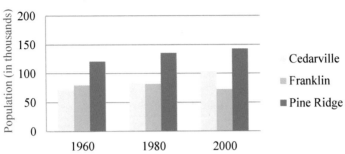

Population Growth by Town, 1960-2000

Pie Charts

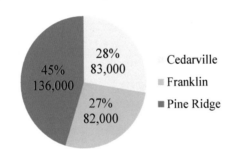

Population Breakdown by Town in 1980

Line Graphs (Middle/Upper Level Only)

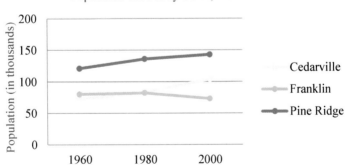

Population Growth by Town, 1960-2000

Data and Probability

Name	Definitions	Example
Range	difference between the biggest and smallest values	In 1, 3, 5, 7, the range is 6
Mean (Average)	sum of data ÷ total number of values	In 1, 3, 5, 7, mean is 4
Median	value that is exactly in the middle of a set of data (or, the avg. of the 2 numbers closest to the middle)	In 1, 4, 6, 11, median is 5
Mode	the value that occurs most frequently	In 1, 1, 3, 5, mode is 1
Probability	number of ways to get a favorable outcome ÷ number of possible outcomes	The probability of a penny landing on "heads" when flipped is 1:2
Probability of Zero	event is impossible	The probability that a six-sided number cube will roll a number greater than 6
Probability of One	event is certain to happen; probability cannot be greater than one	The probability that a six-sided number cube will roll a number between 1 and 6
Mutually exclusive events (Middle/Upper Level Only)	impossible for both events to happen at the same time; can find the chance of one OR the other by adding their probabilities	What is the probability of rolling either the number 5 or the number 3 on a six-sided number cube, with numbers 1 through 6?
Independent events (Middle/Upper Level Only)	events may happen at the same time, but first event does not affect probability of the second; can find the chances of BOTH occurring by multiplying together their probabilities	What is the probability of rolling two even numbers on one roll of two six-sided number cubes?
Dependent events (Middle/Upper Level Only)	one event affects the probability of the other occurring; can find chances of BOTH occurring by determining how the probability of the second is affected by the first and then multiplying their probabilities	Janice picked cards randomly from a standard 52-card deck. She picked her first card and then set it aside, without replacing it, before drawing her second card. What is the probability that both cards were kings?
Probability and geometry (Middle/Upper Level Only)	probability of something happening in a region = Area of specific region ÷ Area of whole figure	Probability of event in blue = Area of blue ÷ Area of white

Venn Diagram	uses overlapping circles that demonstrate relationships between different groups (the **intersection** is where the circles overlap)	Even Numbers: 2, 4, 8, 10, 14 — 6 12 18 — Numbers Divisible by 3: 3, 9, 15, 21, 27
Applying the Counting Principle	to find the number of ways you can complete two or more tasks together, multiply together the number of ways you can complete each task individually	Christy has two scarves and three hats. She wants to pick one scarf and one hat to wear. How many different combinations of one scarf and one hat could she pick? hats × scarves = 2 × 3 = 6
Factorial (Upper Level Only)	the pattern of multiplication where we multiple an integer by all of the positive integers below it	$4! = 4 \times 3 \times 2 \times 1 = 24$
Permutation (Upper Level Only)	a combination of tasks where order matters, solved by $n!$	How many different three-digit numbers can you write using the digits 1, 2, and 3, without repeating any digits? (Answer: $3! = 6$)
Combination (Upper Level Only)	a situation where order does not matter in the arrangement of tasks or objects, solved by $$\frac{n!}{r!\,(n-r)!}$$ r = size of each combination	John, Sue, Marie, and Tom are members of a soccer team. In how many ways can their coach choose two of them to be midfielders? $$\frac{4!}{2!(4-2)!} = 6$$

Stem and Leaf Plots (Middle/Upper Level Only)

- a method for organizing numbers into intervals, making it quick to determine the range, mean, median, and mode of the data.
- Each number in the left-hand column is a **stem,** which represents the tens place of a number.
- Each number next to a stem is a **leaf,** which represents the ones place of a number.

Stem	Leaf
1	1, 2, 6
2	0, 2
3	1
4	5, 6
6	1, 2

Histograms (Upper Level Only)

- a specialized graph frequently used in data analysis to represent a graphical distribution of data, grouped together by values or ranges of values
- by grouping the data together, it displays the **frequency** of those groupings, or the number of times those values r ranges occur in the data set
- also allows us to calculate specific statistical information such as range, mean, median, and mode

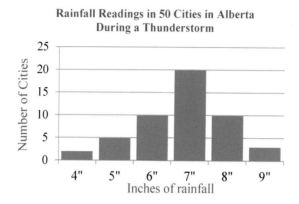

Box and Whisker Graphs (Upper Level Only)

- a graphical way of showing the range, median, and quartiles of a set of data
- each data set has three **quartiles**, which divide the data evenly into four groups: one quarter of the data (25%) is below the first quartile, half (50%) below the second quartile, and three quarters (75%) below the third quartile
- because the second quartile is right in the middle of the data set, it is also the median of the data

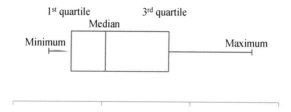

For more information, refer to the Ivy Global ISEE Math Guide (see pages 428-482).

PREPARING FOR YOUR TEST DAY

It is natural to be nervous leading up to your exam. However, if that feeling starts to become overwhelming, here are some strategies that you can use:

1. Relax and slow down.
2. Break your studying into manageable chunks.
3. Sleep and fuel up.
4. Take a break!

The night before the test:

- **Study only lightly.** Don't try to learn anything new.
- Pick out what you are going to wear to the exam—try wearing layers in case the exam room is hotter or colder than you expect.
- Organize everything you need to bring, including your **Admissions Ticket.**
- **Know where the test center is located** and how long it will take to get there.
- Have a nutritious meal and **get plenty of sleep!**

On the morning of the exam:

- Let your adrenaline kick in naturally.
- Eat a good breakfast and stay hydrated; your body needs fuel to endure the test.
- Bring along several pencils and a good eraser.
- Listen carefully to the test proctor's instructions and let the proctor know if you are left-handed so you can sit in an appropriate desk.
- Take a deep breath and remember: you are smart and accomplished! Believe in yourself and you will do just fine.

Made in the USA
Middletown, DE
11 October 2020

20830086R00018